PLAY ON!.

"History provides abundant examples of people whose greatest gift was in redeeming, inspiring, liberating, and nurturing the gifts of others." —*Sonya Rudikoff*

This book is dedicated to Barb King, an incredible woman who embodied the true spirit of play. If you met her, you never forgot her. If you knew her, your life was forever changed.

Steve King and granddaughters; Evalyn, Charlotte and Isabelle

(Cover) Steve and Barb King's granddaughters; Evalyn, Isabelle and Charlotte

Since 1971, Landscape Structures has enhanced

children's lives by fostering and creating inspiring

play experiences while honoring the environment.

Steve King testing the sliding capabilities of the OmniSpin® Spinner
in 10 degrees below zero

CONTENTS

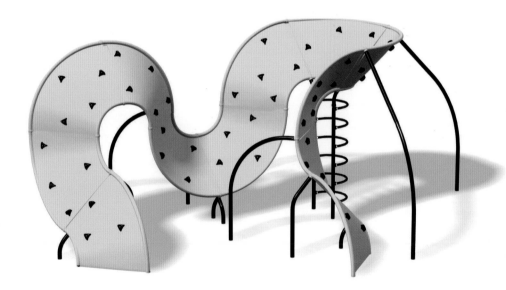

Photography: Steve King
and Mike Bigalke

Design: Michael Lizama

Tire swing illustration by
Draber, 2/23/93

©2013
Landscape Structures Inc.
601 7th Street South
Delano, Minnesota 55328

ISBN 978-0-9887768-0-7
Library of Congress
Control Number 2012955924

This book was typeset in
Whitney and Tarzana-Narrow

Printing: Shapco Printing, Inc.,
Minneapolis, Minnesota on
100# Unisource Velvet Text

Bindery: Midwest Editions,
Minneapolis, Minnesota

It's a happy talent to know how to play. *— Ralph Waldo Emerson*

Barb and Steve King

I don't pretend to be an expert on entrepreneurship. I, along with my late wife, Barb, went on this journey together—sometimes fumbling, sometimes sprinting, but always side-by-side.

Years ago, when Barb and I co-founded Landscape Structures, we saw an opportunity to introduce to the world a new way of thinking about play. As any entrepreneur will tell you, starting, running and nurturing a business is an all-consuming and sometimes scary task. But it's incredibly rewarding, too. In following our passion, we created a paradigm shift on the importance of play in a child's life. That we can positively impact the lives of our future generations is, to me, the ultimate compensation for our hard work.

Along the way, we've had the honor of working with exceptionally talented people. We're humbled by the trust they placed in our vision and the dedication they put into helping propel Landscape Structures forward. Together, we built a thriving business that not only supports our employees financially, but also gives them an outlet to do what they do best: create playgrounds that invite all children to play, learn and grow.

Now, as I reflect on all that has happened since those first whirlwind days in business, I can't help but smile. I am so fortunate to have been able to travel this road with Barb by my side. Together, we managed to build a happy marriage, a loving family and a successful business. We were partners in every sense of the word. I find comfort knowing her legacy continues to this day.

It's a strange thing, how memories can become glossier when you think back on the past. But I, for one, wouldn't have done it any differently. Barb and I built something we believed in, and were fortunate to have a team of people who believed in us. I know Barb would share my pride for how the company has evolved.

I wrote this book to share what I've learned along the way and, hopefully, impart some of that knowledge on the next generation of Landscape Structures owners—its employees. But more so, I wanted to express my profound gratitude for every person who had a part in making this business what it is. We couldn't have done it without you. Thank you.

Steve and Barb playing the Newlywed Game

"Barb was a very special person, and much of her genius was instinctive. Her emotional intelligence was off the charts. She made everyone feel like they were the most important one in the room. When she became sick, we relied on the great team she helped create. The team stepped up and we all helped each other. In a sense, the low point in our company's history became the high point— we were so proud of how people stepped up and pulled together. We didn't want to let her and Steve down." —*Pat Faust, President*

"Some of my best memories are of all the skits that Barb and Steve did to kick off the annual sales meeting each year. How many leaders in an organization would agree to such crazy antics? These have included dressing up in foolish clothes and wigs, acting out the company's history, playing the Newlywed Game, riding in as Snow White and the Seven Dwarfs, dressing up in sumo wrestling outfits, riding/crashing a motorcycle in a motorcycle/skate ramp stunt, dressing in camo and snoring like a bear in a log tunnel, and participating in a dance-off with a glow-in-the-dark jumpsuit! It is so easy to implement fun ideas with owners who have always been willing to say: 'What do you need me to do now?'" —*Amy Jo Madson, Digital Project Manager*

"The relationship that Barb and Steve had represents the heart and soul of Landscape Structures. Their relationship/partnership was incredible. We all know the typical stats associated with husband/wife business partnerships. But Barb and Steve shared 40 years of marriage, and nearly 38 years of working together. If you spent time with them, you understood how special their relationship was. In fact, their partnership provided intrigue for reporters, new hires, business associates and others during the course of all those years. Their motto was always to play in their own sandboxes and not throw sand at each other. While they didn't always agree on everything, there was always an undercurrent of the love they had for each other running through every business decision. That love for each other, for kids, for life is a big part of what has made Landscape Structures successful. How fortunate are those who experienced the incredible team of Barb and Steve." —*Lynn Pinoniemi, Director of Marketing*

This is the real secret of life—to be completely engaged with what you are doing in the here and now. And instead of calling it work, realize it is play. *— Alan Wilson Watts*

CHAPTER 1 Past, Present and Future

"As a boy, Steve was very energetic and always had to have something to do. He loved doing outdoor work, and I remember him telling me, 'I'm never going to work in an office.' Reading books wasn't his favorite thing— he'd rather be outside doing something."

Esther King, Steve's mom

I was born in northern Minnesota, but I grew up in Iowa. There were five siblings in my family, and I was the second born. I'm a preacher's kid, but no one ever confused me with an angel. My father died when he was 83, but my mother, who is 97, is still active. Her mother lived to be 101!

We lived in many different small towns in Iowa. My folks were usually without money, so if I wanted anything I had to work for it. I had many jobs at an early age: mowing lawns, delivering newspapers, selling Christmas cards, doing yard work, working as a church janitor. After I graduated from high school in Dumont, Iowa, I went on to college. I spent my first year at Westmar College in Le Mars, Iowa. I didn't do well there—they told me they'd forgive all my traffic tickets and send me away with no hard feelings if I agreed to take a career aptitude test and not return to Westmar. It was one of the best things that ever happened to me. The test led me to get a degree in landscape architecture from Iowa State University in Ames, Iowa.

Meeting Barb

During my sophomore year at Iowa State, I had a blind date with a fellow student named Barbara Olson. She was born in Illinois, but her family had moved around, and she graduated from high school in Muscatine, Iowa. We didn't hit it off at first, but a year later I met her again. We went to a football game, and the rest is history. We were married before she graduated with her degree in home economics. Even after we married, I continued to work many jobs. Other kids would go out to party, but I said I was going to work. It didn't bother me at all. I knew I had to work to get what we needed, and I had a school loan to pay off. Barb was like that too. As the oldest of two girls in a doctor's family, it wasn't necessary for her to find work, but after we were married, we needed her income and she got a check-out job in a grocery store.

I was and still am motivated to look at work as a pathway. We got Barb through school, learned a work ethic and realized that work is not a bad thing—especially if you're using it to follow your destiny.

After Barb finished school, I wanted to move to the Pacific Northwest, where I had a job offer. Barb, however, was offered a job in food and nutrition at Pillsbury in Minneapolis. They offered her work testing recipes and generating material for cookbooks. So we packed up and moved to the Twin Cities.

I found a job as a landscape architect specializing in park planning for a consulting firm in Minneapolis. I'm not sure why the design firm trusted me with anything, inexperienced kid that I was, but in 1969 I was assigned to a playground design project for the City of Minneapolis. I wanted to try out my continuous play concept (see sidebar), which I was convinced would facilitate the development of social, mental and physical skills. The city's project manager was skeptical of the approach and of the building material I wanted to use, wood, but after hours of discussion he said, "What the heck, let's try it. We have 400 parks—we'll try it on one."

After the structure was built in Northeast Minneapolis, the neighbors loved it. It was amazing to watch the kids play on the structure. They played in ways I didn't expect and some ways I did. If it had been larger, it would have been an even bigger success. People from other neighborhoods called the City of Minneapolis wanting their own playground just like it.

"I remember Steve starting out by making simple benches
and picnic tables that he built in his garage. His clients,
mainly landscape architects, were looking for that type
of item, which they couldn't find in catalogs. From there,
it continued to grow." —*Bill Sanders, Landscape Architect*

In the beginning, there was continuous play

Zachman Homes' first playstructure

The continuous play concept describes an outdoor learning environment where play components are connected or functionally linked to provide a variety of play challenges on the same structure. Playstructures designed this way help develop fine and gross motor skills, social skills, planning skills, teamwork and even conflict-resolution skills. This can all happen in a relatively small space where both supervision and maintenance are easier. A successful playstructure design must provide challenges for all users.

When I was a landscape architectural student at Iowa State University in the mid-1960s, playgrounds had standard freestanding metal equipment: swings, slides, spinners, monkey bars and jungle gyms, all designed for older kids. The playground was typically over asphalt, gravel or dirt. Isolated from one another and spread out over a lot of space, these components didn't offer many choices, but at least they were challenging for older kids.

I was eager to learn more about play, so I decided to observe kids at the Child Development Department at Iowa State University. It didn't take long for me to realize that the children didn't play in the way that traditional playgrounds led you to believe. Kids didn't like standing in line to go down the slide or use the swings—they wanted to be doing something. What they really wanted were group activities: manipulating sand and water, playing follow the leader and tag, collecting stones and sticks, and finding hiding places inside cardboard boxes. I remember seeing three girls who made up a course they followed around the play area without touching the ground. They had spontaneously invented their own game and created their own challenges.

The behavior of the kids got me thinking. Why not design a playstructure that fits the way children like to play? Why not try to combine playground activities in a continuous flow with options along the way? I could plan a structure that enabled them to play together with a variety of levels of challenges that would satisfy a broad range of ages. They could make their own choices and move from one activity to another without ever touching the ground. The type of playground design that I envisioned would actually save space by combining activities, and it would encourage kids to interact with each other and collaboratively decide what to do next. It would be a more interesting and creative playground that featured an array of interconnected bridges, climbers, slides and ladders. I eventually called this approach the continuous play concept.

From 1966 to 1967, as part of my final project for my degree in landscape architecture, I designed an open space for a townhouse development in a neighboring town. All the residents, including many families, got really excited about designing a playstructure that embodied this continuous play concept. I presented my plan to my advisor, who was the head of the department. He looked it over and heard me out. Then he gave me bad news. "It's a great presentation," he said, "but your design solution won't work. If they're all playing together, the kids will push and shove—they won't cooperate." I responded by talking about the importance of playgrounds giving kids a variety of challenges and practice in conflict resolution and teamwork—all the things they will face when they grow up. I told him I could put all of those challenges and opportunities in one small space. I wouldn't need the half acre that traditional playgrounds required. "It's an interesting concept, Steve, but you're asking for trouble," he said. "Your project is supposed to reflect reality." He gave me a C+, which shocked me. I was devastated. But I had an attitude then (and still do now). I thought, "I'll show you."

Now nearly every new playstructure produced by every manufacturer is based on the continuous play concept, and you can find it at schools, parks, fast-food restaurants, childcare centers, places of worship, theme parks and even on the roofs of buildings. The concept completely changed the industry and the way we think about play, even 45 years later.

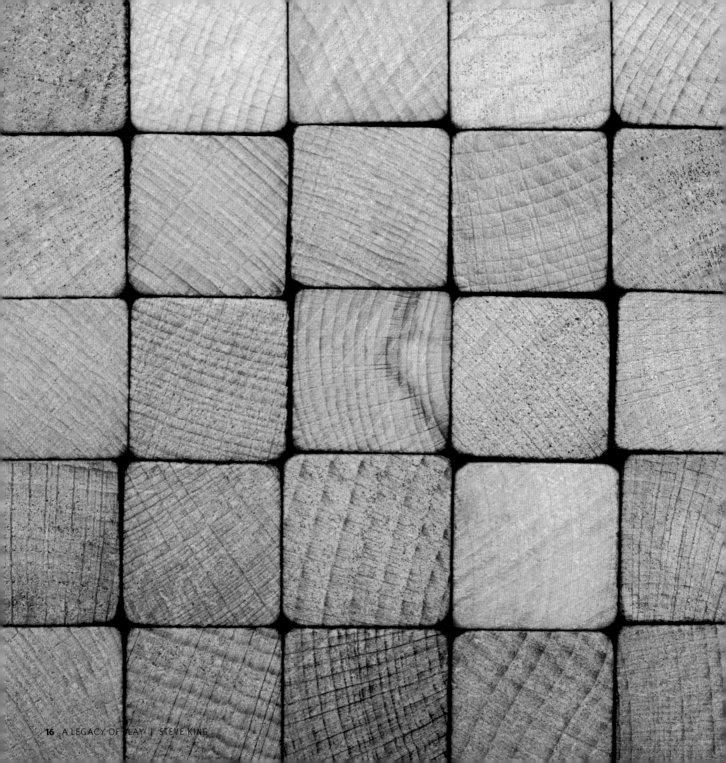

The company takes shape

That first playground project in Minneapolis went well, and we started thinking there might be a business here. I quit my job and started my own site planning firm, King Associates, in 1969. King Associates did well, but most of the work was not related to playgrounds. One of my clients, Zachman Homes, was building a townhouse project and I suggested the model home needed a playstructure for the kids. They liked the idea, and thus the first playstructure built under my name that utilized the continuous play concept was born (see sidebar on page 15). This pioneering playstructure got a lot of attention, and soon other developers wanted one. When the City of St. Louis Park, Minnesota, asked me to design a playground, we knew we had something. I gave them a guaranteed price of $10,000, and I hung around during its installation to make sure the contractor did his job well.

In early 1971, the city told us we had to move our business out of our home. We later learned that our neighbors didn't like hearing us sawing wood late at night and piling the lumber up in our front yard. I wonder why?

One of my King Associates clients owned a warehouse with a vacancy, and he offered us rent-free space if I continued to do work for him. Soon after, in April 1971, we incorporated Landscape Structures to design and build these playstructures. We chose the name to more accurately reflect our business focus. We were broke and borrowed $1,000 to incorporate the new business and buy basic tools. We had a dream to bring this new concept to the marketplace and suddenly we were in business. The continuous play idea that I planted in 1966 and germinated three years later had at last blossomed. We didn't know if this concept would become a success or not, but we were going to give it everything we had. King Associates continued site planning projects for a few years to help fund Landscape Structures' growth.

I bought some of my treated wood from a local lumberyard, and the company president, Ben Swayze, liked us and wanted to help. He thought of us as his kids. He came to our house at least once a week for several weeks and taught Barb how to keep the books and analyze financial statements. He also told us we weren't charging enough for our products and urged us to significantly increase our prices, which was great advice.

Early redwood playstructures

All this time Barb worked part-time for Landscape Structures doing the administrative work at home and worked full-time for Pillsbury. For a while, the hardest part of our job was telling callers we couldn't take any more orders until we caught up and resolved our cash flow problems. Sometimes we took the phone off the hook because we had more business than we could handle. We had no credit, so everything was purchased with cash. Many days I worked 16 to 18 hours, designing, selling, building and installing. Barb worked five years for Landscape Structures before she ever got a paycheck.

I believe one of the reasons we were successful as both husband/wife and business partners is that we each had our own sandbox. She was the software and I was the hardware—it takes both to make it work. I focused my energies on product development, while Barb focused on running the company-wide operations.

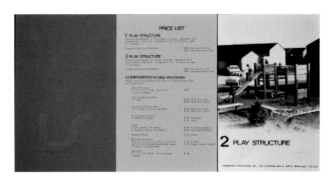

Early Landscape Structures catalog

In the early 1970s, there were only a handful of major players in the play equipment business. We had the only modular panelized wood structures, and I soon added other play components. When one of our larger competitors started to offer similar structures, I realized the value of continuous play. I really believed we were on to something.

As time went by, I became concerned about the chemicals in the treated wood coming into contact with children. By the mid-1970s, we converted to high-quality redwood, which didn't need to be treated.

Steve, Barb and Erin King

"As kids, we had a beautiful redwood playground in our front yard. It had monkey bars, a tire swing and a fireman's pole. We were the neighborhood park—kids came from around the neighborhood to play there. My parents sold the house when I was in my twenties, that playground was still there. It holds a lot of happy memories."—*Erin King, Barb and Steve's daughter*

Financial hurdles

We might have been on to something, but we needed money to keep the business going. We went to banks, venture capitalists and friends of friends, trying to borrow money and invest in the business. We had no background in finance. The bankers kept turning us down. Finally we found Dave Cleveland at Riverside Banks in Minneapolis. He heard our story and must have thought we were crazy. "Steve, you have more guts than brains," he said. Incredibly, he loaned us money and helped us get further funding from the Small Business Administration.

> "I make loans based on honesty, integrity and work habits, which are the only ways you can judge entrepreneurs. Riverside Banks had a reputation for providing loans to entrepreneurs and due to this reputation had a constant stream of prospects. I probably turned down more business loan applications than any banker in America. I remember thinking that Barb and Steve made quite a team." —*Dave Cleveland, Banker*

Then in late 1971, Barb's department closed at Pillsbury. Barb went on unemployment, and two weeks later she told me she was pregnant. Our daughter, Erin, came along in 1972. Now we were a family without any income. I was building playgrounds, but we still didn't have a dime with which to do anything.

That was when we felt the personal sacrifices that entrepreneurship demanded. We ate popcorn and macaroni and cheese, Spam® on a good day—that was about it. I vividly remember still feeling hungry after dinner. Neighbors cooked us meals and brought us leftovers. Our friends went out for dinner and movies, which we couldn't afford, and the high cost of gasoline kept us from taking trips. Our home emptied of furniture, sold off to raise money. Our house was foreclosed on several times, but somehow we were able to make interest payments to keep it. The sacrifices seemed so great, and lasted so long. People around us couldn't understand what we were going through or why.

Our need for money was so immediate that I had to insist on cash for everything. We had customers but couldn't afford to sell to them or reinvest in the business. I remember telling one customer, a real estate developer for whom I was building a playground, "I'm not sending an invoice. Please have your check ready when I finish. On the way home, I'll use the money to buy more material for the next job."

Barb and I were in a real financial bind. We sat down together at the kitchen table and realized it was ridiculous for me to keep working up to 18 hours a day—we had a child to raise. Our annual sales were about $100,000, but all we had in our house were two chairs, a table, a settee and two beds. We had so many yard sales to raise cash, there wasn't anything left to sell. The IRS was after us for back taxes, too. I'll never forget Barb telling the IRS representative that this was the cheapest—and only—loan we could get. He had never heard that excuse before but was impressed by her honesty and gave us more time to pay off the "loan."

Those were tough times. The pace of work was literally killing me. I was exhausted and often felt light headed. My weight dropped 10 or 15 pounds and customers told me I didn't look healthy. I thought I had the flu, so I went to a doctor who told me to stop working. I couldn't stop. We were living hand to mouth, using what cash we had to buy wood for the next project. Our idea of long-term planning was figuring out what we were going to eat at the next meal.

We decided we had to think hard about getting real jobs, so we flipped a coin. Heads, we get jobs. Tails, I'd spend all my time finding money for the business. It came up heads. We thought about it, and decided to make it two out of three. That indicated how we really felt. We wanted to be in business, and we weren't ready yet to give up on our dream. We had a great idea, just no money—like a lot of entrepreneurs. We couldn't fail because we had no backup.

When I resumed looking for money in 1974, the banks and the Small Business Administration wouldn't lend us any more. So I spent the next few weeks meeting with venture capitalists. All kinds of investors saw me, and they all said they weren't interested. Finally, after one of them again turned me down, one person there said I should go next door and make a pitch to the Young Presidents Organization. "I'll introduce you," this investor said. "Maybe they will be interested."

He introduced me to Gerry Rauenhorst, who appeared to be the leader of the Young Presidents Organization. I gave my pitch. Gerry listened and said, "I like this kid. I'll chip in $5,000." Then he pointed to other members of the group. "And so will you, and you and you." He raised a total of $40,000, and Gerry added another $10,000 as a loan. In return, their newly formed venture capital organization, Executive Venture Capital, wanted to own 50 percent of our company and a seat on the board.

Barb and I discussed the deal that night and came to the conclusion that owning 50 percent of something is better than having 100 percent of nothing. We now had a partner and could get credit from suppliers and hire more people. (We eventually paid the investment partnership back in 1990.) We started selling one, and sometimes two, playstructures a week. Things suddenly started turning around.

Redwood playstructure from 1979

Profitability arrives

At the same time, we ran out of space in the warehouse, and were storing wood outside in the parking lot. It didn't take long for the city inspector to figure out what I was doing. A guy showed up from the zoning department and told me I couldn't store wood out in the parking lot. We had nowhere else to store it. Then another King Associates client, a landscape nursery owner, Gus Gustafson, from Delano, Minnesota, stepped in to help. They built a pole building for us that included an outdoor storage area for lumber on four acres and only asked that we make the mortgage payments. We moved to the Delano area in 1974 and have been here ever since.

In 1976, our sales nearly reached $1 million, and we realized that we had made a profit and owed taxes. Our accountant Dan Vaughn told me something that has stayed with me: "Steve, be thankful you're paying taxes. Many people out there pay no taxes because they have no profits. It's hard to like taxes, but the fact remains that if you're paying taxes, you're making money and keeping more of it than the government does." Landscape Structures has been profitable every year since then. I believe we have a much better business today because of the hardships we went through at the beginning.

Profitability arrived just in time. We adopted our son, Adam, as a two-year-old from Korea in 1978. He adjusted very well and became an important part of our lives.

"We were aware that they worked long hours, but Mom and Dad made a big effort to be involved in our lives. They always tried to have one or both of them go to our sporting events—they made a real effort to show up."—*Adam King, Steve and Barb's son*

Redwood playstructure from 1991

Forming a company culture

By the end of the 1970s, we had developed our business philosophy. We were, and have always been, focused on the best product design, customer service and quality. We set the standard, which employees learned and adopted. Barb and I always had an informal approach to managing our people—we gave people authority and responsibility, and we made sure we didn't give responsibility without authority. That's been the hallmark of our business culture ever since. Anyone could come talk to us, anytime. We became dedicated to that style of management. Employees think of us as a family.

"It was clear that Steve's business ethics were of the highest caliber. The product quality was first-rate. The company was the class of the industry, and I'm not surprised at its later success." —*Bob Wooters, Venture Capitalist*

This marked the start of our company culture, which began simply by taking pride in what we do. Since those early years, we've shown it in our eagerness to work, our understanding of everyone's role in our business and in the world, and in the importance we place in improving our products. Employees know that if a weld is rough, we grind it smooth, and if the paint hasn't adhered, we go back and do it right. Another part of our culture was and is the openness of our communication. Anyone could talk to us and to each other. Barb didn't even have a door on her office. Everyone knows how much money we make and all the other important information about our company. Building a culture is a hard thing. But when it's done well, the culture is easy to distinguish from that of other companies.

Bringing in sales representatives was a big step in our growth. In 1974, I attended my first trade show in Minnesota and set up our display. The guy next to me was selling old tires for use in playgrounds. He was Jack Gleason, the owner of TireToys. He asked if we were interested in selling his stuff, and I said it wouldn't fit into our product line. Then he said, "I might be interested in selling your products." We brought him on as one of our first sales reps. He was one of the best sales reps out there— hardworking, honest and serving customers well. Jack's the epitome of customer service. Now he's retired, and his daughter Moira continues to manage a very successful business, NuToys Leisure Products, Inc. They're our largest sales organization.

"Partnering with Landscape Structures has been a real pleasure, and I feel like one of the luckiest men on earth to have found them. It was one of the great lucky turns of my life." —*Jack Gleason, NuToys Leisure Products, Inc., Retired Sales Representative*

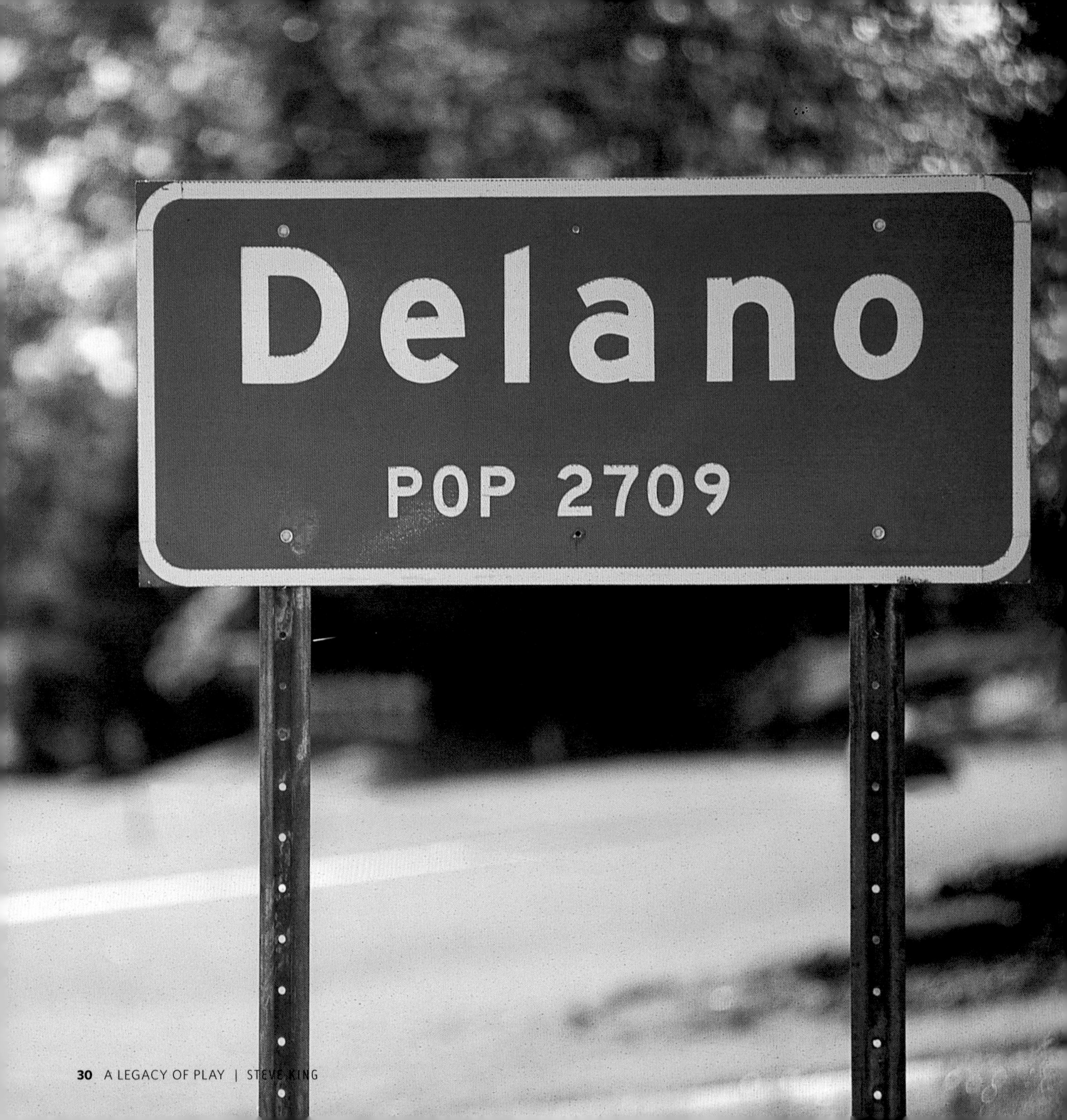
Delano
POP 2709

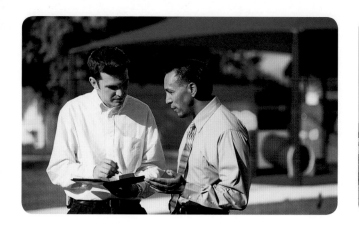

Sales reps are crucial to our success, and they are our face to the customer. They sell more than our products—they also sell the culture of Landscape Structures. We take pride in having the best sales organizations in the industry. They add initiative, drive, dedication, personality, intelligence, and attention to detail and customer service. As holders of an exclusive geographic sales territory, our sales reps are independent, and we treat them as valued partners who have an inside knowledge of the industry. We know that if our top 10 reps stopped selling for us, we'd be out of business in short order. And my relationships with many sales reps have grown beyond business connections to close personal bonds that will last a lifetime.

Landscape Structures grew steadily during the late 1970s and 1980s. In 1981 we moved to the industrial park in Delano. Our first building there was twice expanded during the 1980s. We steadily introduced new products and brought new materials to the industry.

Mexico Forge catalog at the time of acquisition

A difficult acquisition

In 1984 we made our first business acquisition—Mexico Forge, a metal playground equipment manufacturing company in Pennsylvania that was slightly larger than we were. The combination gave us annual sales of nearly $14 million. I knew by then that wood was on its way out as a playstructure material: it required a lot of maintenance, and high-quality redwood was becoming expensive and hard to find. Environmentalists were pointing out that old-growth redwood trees were vanishing from the forest and needed to be preserved. With the acquisition came PlayBooster®, a metal playsystem utilizing the continuous play concept. We made many improvements to that product line, and in 1986 we introduced the new PlayBooster, which really moved us ahead. It remains our most popular playsystem today.

We had no idea, though, that the Mexico Forge acquisition would cause us many frustrations and headaches. But it was a great learning experience. The problem was the different cultures of the companies. We gave employees the authority and responsibility to think independently—quite different from their union shop. Mexico Forge

was focused on short-term thinking. We were frustrated when we discovered that people there could do only certain kinds of work and had no attachment to the products they made. Trying to meld these two company cultures just didn't work. So in 1986 we moved all the Mexico Forge operations to Minnesota, and offered jobs to all the Pennsylvania employees. No employees moved. When we received the Mexico Forge equipment, it had been vandalized and some of it couldn't be used.

We certainly learned from that experience, and in time we came to think that we were invincible in our knowledge of the industry. Big mistake. We decided to start manufacturing backyard playground equipment—how could backyard equipment be so different from the manufacturing and marketing of the structures we were already selling to parks and schools? We thought it was the same thing, just on a smaller scale. That was a terribly wrong assumption. There were different safety standards, techniques of marketing and materials that we had to use. Everything was different, and we weren't prepared. Within a couple of years, we closed that part of the business. We did the same thing when we got into the trucking business. Both were expensive lessons, and both were common mistakes entrepreneurs make.

Now I mentor young entrepreneurs about the need to focus, get good at something and earn the right to move to a different product or channel. People often assume they have the talent and money to learn two different businesses at once. But I have learned that is not true. You pick the best, focus and hire the right people to get it done. You surround yourself with people who do their jobs better than you would. Entrepreneurs who can't give up some responsibilities will see their businesses die. Instead, figure out exactly how you can best contribute to the success of the business, and focus on that. Every day I told myself I had to focus—playgrounds were our business, we had to earn the right to move into new markets. I wish someone would have beaten that message into my head earlier.

Growth at home and overseas

We found our first international sales representatives, Kotobuki, in 1982. They were a Japanese firm that had already visited our competitors—all bigger than we were—but thought we made the best products. They told us they wanted to sell our products. We didn't know anything about shipping to Japan or how to navigate the currency exchange rate, but we learned fast and they helped us along. They loved Barb—women in Japan at that time didn't often hold senior positions in business, and they were impressed. "How's President Barbara?" they'd ask. The company has remained loyal to us ever since.

After Japan we expanded to other Asian countries—Hong Kong and Singapore. We've built good representation in Europe. We also sell in Mexico, Canada, Australia, the Middle East and India.

Landscape Structures receives Japan's G-Mark International Design Award for design of an AdventureScape, 1998

Hong Kong Gold Coast Hotel, Hong Kong, China

Larne Town Park Play Area,
Larne, Northern Ireland

Meanwhile, our sales steadily rose—they hit $15 million in 1988, and $30 million by 1994. We had nearly 200 employees and were shipping our products throughout the United States and 17 foreign countries.

An important milestone came for us in 1990. Years earlier, in 1974, we had sold half of our business to a venture capital group for $40,000. We were desperate in those early years, and we had to get our hands on money to keep our dream alive. The money we raised by selling that 50 percent equity provided for our survival. In 1990 we completed a buyout of our partner, an investor and friend named Bob Wooters, who took over from the original investors. I'll never forget the celebration we had when the company returned to our sole ownership.

Barb and I hit a peak during the early 1990s. Finally, we didn't have to struggle for groceries or worry about the next meal. We realized we were in it for the long term and we could sometimes take vacations. The business had matured and we were earning more than enough money. We were named Minnesota's

Entrepreneurs of the Year by Ernst and Young and by *Inc. Magazine,* and we were voted into the National Institute of Entrepreneurs. Not much later, Barb was chosen as the Small Business Administration's "Small Business Person of the Year." Barb was also busy with various local organizations, including the National Association of Women Business Owners (NAWBO), of which she became president. Landscape Structures became a charter member of the International Play Equipment Manufacturers Association (IPEMA), which was established in 1995, and I later served as president and board member.

Those were really good times. It was gratifying to see that we were feeding hundreds of people in the families of our employees and reps. That felt good.

Also during the 1990s, new safety standards and the Americans with Disabilities Act changed the industry, and all of a sudden public playgrounds had to conform to new safety and accessibility standards. Many playgrounds had to be modified or replaced, and all manufacturers saw substantial growth during this time.

JT's Grommet Island Beach
Park & Playground for Every
"Body," Virginia Beach, Virginia

"Steve and Barb are iconic figures in our industry and represent such a great American success story. They embody so much of what's so great about our country."—*Ewing Philbin, Principal, Ross Recreation Equipment Company, Inc.*

A position of leadership in the industry today

Our sales exceeded $100 million in 2008, and we grew into a company with more than 300 employees working on our Delano campus of six buildings. In 2004 we created an employee stock ownership plan (ESOP), part of our succession plan; Barb and I told employees of our intention to ultimately have the company be 100 percent employee owned. We have given more than $2 million a year in profits to buy company stock for employees. As the company grows, the number of shares that employees own also grows. I think of our business success as a tribute to Barb, who died in 2008, at the age of 61, after several months of battling cancer. In her final years she worked more hours than I did—she loved it here. She still had the fire in her belly and felt challenged at Landscape Structures. She repeatedly shared our company motto; if we do good work, good results will follow. Our company culture was her creation, and her passing was a terribly sad loss to me, our family and to the Landscape Structures family.

It gratified me tremendously that more than a thousand people came to honor and remember Barb at her memorial service. In 2010, we dedicated the Barb King Inspiration Park in Delano to her memory. Landscape Structures donated the equipment. The park has a unique design, never to be duplicated, and it uses a high percentage of recycled materials. I think she'd be pleased.

I think she would also be pleased that as of the end of 2012, employees now own 100 percent of Landscape Structures. Employees are working harder than ever to bring the company continued success. We are the only U.S. playground equipment company that is owned by employees, which is reflected in the care employees take to meet customer needs. I'm confident that employees will continue the legacy that Barb and I started.

Barb King
Inspiration Park,
Delano, Minnesota

Mobius® Climber

Reflections on what we've built

What we've built—and this makes me feel enormously proud—is a premier playground equipment company. Our culture and employee ownership, the heart of our operations, are tremendous contributors to our success that cannot be copied. Employees are passionate about their jobs and believe in our shared mission to make the best products on the market.

We've earned many awards and honors. Some are tremendously important to me: the Tekne Green Award in 2008; designation as Minnesota Work-Life Champion and Minnesota Waste Wise Leader that same year; and the Star Tribune Top Work Places in 2010, 2011 and 2012. I was named a Landscape Architecture Fellow by the American Society of Landscape Architects in 2004—the first manufacturer ever so designated—an honor that goes to less than 3 percent of the people in my profession.

From the very beginning, our commitment to quality never wavered. Many competitor products' look similar to ours, but it is the attention to the details that make the difference. Our sales representatives are the best and most knowledgeable in the business. When customers need a part, we get it to them within 48 hours. That's just part of our commitment to our customers.

I would like to think that Landscape Structures would have thrived anywhere, but Delano has been a terrific home for us. We're now the largest private employer in the area. A lot of places would like to have a business like Landscape Structures. Moving here was a good thing to do. We have access to great employees and enough space for our needs. Here we can stay on the same campus and grow. A recent growth opportunity was our acquisition of Pebble-Flex® LLC, a company that manufactures PebbleFlex®, a bond-in-place surfacing installed under and around playground equipment, and AquaFlex®, surfacing designed especially for water parks and pool decks. The acquisition gave us diversification and the opportunity to be a one-stop shop for our customers. The product is well accepted in our industry for its performance. This time, I believe, their culture will be a good fit with our business.

PebbleFlex®
Safety Surfacing

"A few times I asked Barb why she didn't have a reserved parking spot near the entrance to the building. She said, 'Whoever gets here first should get it.' She was always open to talk with anyone." —*Gene Keck, Retrofit Engineer*

What's in store

When I think about how our industry has changed, the growing involvement of lawyers has to be at the top of the list. We've had to invest a great deal of money to defend ourselves from questionable lawsuits, and the attorneys are the only ones getting rich (see Challenges and Opportunities Chapter 3).

There are interesting challenges ahead in the future of playgrounds. In the last few years, many organizations have been examining the balance between play value and benefits to kids versus safety. Many researchers have concluded that playgrounds need more challenges, and that a certain amount of risk benefits children. The emphasis on safety is out of balance because it limits the developmental opportunities for kids, especially older ones. The Health and Safety Executive published in the U.K. recently got it right in declaring, "Play is great for children's well-being and development. When planning and providing play opportunities, the goal is not to eliminate risk, but to weigh up the risks and benefits. No child will learn about risk if he is wrapped in cotton wool."

We increasingly see headlines about playgrounds that have been "dumbed down" in an overreaching concern for children's safety. I hope policy makers will take note and support guidelines and legislation that give kids the same play opportunities and challenges they enjoyed 50 years ago. I say this as someone who was a charter member of the American Society for Testing and Materials (ASTM), a committee responsible for developing performance safety standards for public playgrounds. For 20 years, I chaired a task group of that committee, and now I'm not sure that was time well spent. We have not significantly reduced the number of playground accidents, but we most certainly have reduced the play value of those playgrounds, especially for older kids. The change we need must begin with tort

Lake Rebecca Park Reserve,
Rockford, Minnesota

Harvest Park, Mapleton, Utah

reform that eliminates frivolous lawsuits. Organizations that set safety standards should revise their guidelines to restore the balance between risk and safety. We need to start calling playgrounds what they really are: outdoor learning environments.

If all that someday falls into place, I look forward to playgrounds of the future that are more challenging as well as having the qualities of being available to all users, multi-generational in appeal, and manufactured from composite materials not yet developed. I can see 20-foot-high towers, some with elevators, high slides, cable rides, new kinds of climbers, electronics and lots of cables. The continuous play concept we began with was just a start in this industry—we have come a long way, but we also have a long way to go.

I will continue my position as chairman of the board at Landscape Structures. As for my personal plans for the future, I hope to spend more time helping other entrepreneurs, fly fishing, traveling and spending more time with my family. As for family, our daughter, Erin, attended college and traveled extensively. She received a master's degree in Chinese medicine and started a practice in acupuncture and herbal medicine. She's currently furthering her studies in Ayurvedic (Indian) medicine. She and her husband, Mark, live in Seattle, Washington. By the time he was 13, our son, Adam was showing a great interest in cooking. He is now an executive chef at Café Lurcat in Minneapolis, Minnesota, and was one of the youngest chefs to manage a top restaurant in the region. He and his wife, Tara, have three daughters, Isabelle, Charlotte and Evalyn.

I will continue to work in Africa to help villages become self-sufficient and sustaining (see the Community Chapter 5 for my work there). I intend to continue giving back by committing a significant percent of my income to charitable causes and by helping others achieve success.

Both Barb and I established scholarships for deserving college students: the Barbara A. King Scholarship Endowment for Innovation and Entrepreneurship rewards students in the Landscape Architectural program at Iowa State University, and the Steven G. King Play Environments Scholarship benefits students who design unique play environments.

I've learned a lot on our journey and I now enjoy sharing my expertise and experience with others. Barb and I learned the hard way, but we earned our rewards. Now one of the things I enjoy most is helping start-up businesses become successful. We didn't have that kind of mentor when we started, but many people helped us in small segments along the way. And I am very grateful for their help.

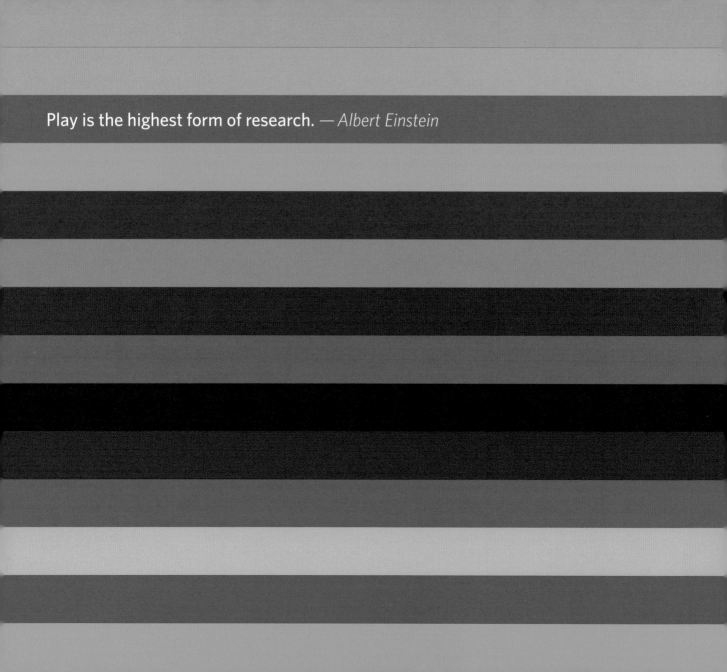

Play is the highest form of research. — *Albert Einstein*

CHAPTER 2 Innovation

North Carolina Aquarium at Fort Fisher,
Kure Beach, North Carolina

"Landscape Structures' success has been made possible because of the original vision Steve had—developing the concept of continuous play. Steve and Barb created a great company that lives and breathes their core values and work ethic. I am so proud to be a part of Landscape Structures!"—*Jean Hayes, Marketing Events Specialist*

From our origination of the concept of continuous play in 1966, Landscape Structures has based its success on a steady flow of innovation.

In our products, we have introduced new materials and play components involving climbing nets, cable, track rides, tree houses, talk tubes, trolley rides, corkscrew climbers and play panels, many of which are accessible to children with special needs. Our PlayBooster® playsystem revolutionized playgrounds by introducing post-and-clamp construction, which made an unlimited number of configurations possible. Back in 1985, AdventureScape was the first composite playsystem for ages 2 to 5. With Evos® in 2007 we introduced gyroscopic play and the pure arch. The design of that playsystem evolved from our certainty that the market was ready for equipment not made from posts and decks.

At first, I designed most of our innovations. I'd walk through a shopping center and see some detail on a guard rail or furnishing, and pretty soon I'd incorporate that detail into our equipment. One time, I looked at the partitions in an airport bathroom and realized that the same polyethylene material could work as activity panels in our playstructures. From that notion, we introduced Permalene®. Today our design process is sophisticated and collaborative. Design ideas can come from all over, internally and externally. There's no single genius saying, "Let's do this next." Collaboration is part of the process. When we learn about a societal trend like childhood obesity, we discuss what we can do to contribute to the solution. When someone has an idea, they sketch it out and show it to others. What we work on next is based on group consensus.

(Clockwise from upper left)
Spacenet®, SpringRing® Bouncer, Sway Fun® Glider,
Mobius® Climber, Skatewave® modular skatepark system

"Landscape Structures isn't one of those Wall Street conglomerates where the bottom line is money. They build products that intrigue children, get them to play and have been designed with fresh eyes. The only discouraging part of working with them is when Landscape Structures develops a great product, and a year later the copies start appearing." —*Eric O'Brien, Principal, M.E. O'Brien & Sons, Inc.*

As Landscape Structures grows, more and more people have a voice in our design decisions. We have teams of people from different disciplines collaborating on the product development process: design, engineering, testing, manufacturing, marketing, sales and packaging. From this process comes our next great product line. The gratifying thing is that many of our designs become industry standards. Sometimes it appears that we do research and development for the entire playground equipment industry.

Our list of innovative product introductions is long: the first fitness trail system in 1977; the first multi-age play event, the SpringRing® Bouncer, in 1996; we introduced modular steel skatepark equipment, Skatewave® in 2001; the debut of Spacenet® in 2003; Mobius®, the first playground climber integrating art and play in 2005; the first natural-looking climbing rocks for preschoolers in 2010; and many more firsts too numerous to mention. We premiere 10 to 20 new products each year. At first there were only a few simple things kids could do on our structures. Now there are many more choices. Some of our structures are pre-configured, but most are customized for the customer.

We're especially proud of our innovations in designing inclusive playstructures. In 1993, after the passage of the federal Americans with Disabilities Act (ADA), I served on the Federal Access Board's Recreation Access Advisory Committee as the group's only representative from a playground equipment manufacturer. Nobody then really understood how to make playgrounds accessible. Once at a public hearing, I asked a man in a wheelchair how he gets in and out of bed and how he uses a bathroom and shower. He laughed and said, "Nobody ever asks us questions like that," and he explained. I learned that many people with disabilities can scoot up stairs, and I watched them transfer from wheelchairs to other kinds of furnishings. I was impressed and incorporated those observations into our research and development. We were the first to design a transfer module into our playstructures; we also introduced the Sway Fun® glider, a multi-user glider that was the first of its kind to be accessible to children and adults in wheelchairs.

Metropolitan Multi-Service Center,
City of Houston, Texas

In the materials we use to build our playstructures, we've revolutionized the industry. We started building with pressure-treated pine, but we didn't like the toxicity of the chemicals used to preserve the wood. Then redwood became our material of choice for many years. Eventually the quality and quantity of the wood available to us diminished, and in 1981 we introduced Alumacore®, an extruded aluminum post with redwood facing.

At about the same time, and before anyone in the industry knew anything about it, we began coating decks and steel parts—anything that kids touched and could cut themselves on or burn themselves on during hot, sunny days—with TenderTuff™ coating, otherwise known as PVC (polyvinyl chloride). I became interested in PVC when I was fiddling with my freezer—I noticed that my hand didn't stick to the shelving. It took a lot of training and education to help sales reps and customers understand the benefits of PVC as a coating: it provides softness to the touch, abrasion resistance and can moderate temperature. In 1981 I took our samples to the National Recreation and Park Association (NRPA) convention in Minneapolis. One competitor came over to our display and felt the TenderTuff samples. "You've lost your mind," he stated. "It won't work." I love it when people tell me it won't work. Nothing motivates me more. Three years later, everyone in the industry was using this material (some of the early PVCs contained toxic chemicals, which Landscape Structures never used). TenderTuff is an idea that changed the industry and, like our continuous play concept, it's an industry standard.

(Left) TenderTuff™ coating process

(Above) TenderTuff™ coated steering wheels

(Right) Alumacore® post

Cypress Creek Lakes
Recreation Center,
Cypress, Texas

Welcome

Our newest twist in materials has come from concrete, which is a big deal now. It's part of our emphasis on nature-inspired and sensory play, which has led us to come up with new components and activities to incorporate into our play areas. The creative potential of this material inspired us to bring our concrete production in-house, which has greatly improved the creativity and quality of our work. We are the only playground equipment company with an in-house concrete plant. Concrete is a material that allows us to duplicate various features of nature while following safety standards. We've used concrete to fashion rocks, animals and sculptures of all types. Our team of artists and sculptors are able to give our customers what they want and children what they need—sensory stimulation and a heightened sense of being outdoors. We can make concrete surfaces colorful and smooth or rough, whatever is needed to reflect Mother Nature.

Products created
and manufactured
in our concrete
facility

"Barb and Steve created a great culture at Landscape Structures. Their character, leadership and innovative approaches have inspired many of us. I am fortunate to have worked closely with Steve on the product development side of the business for over 20 years. I have always been impressed by his design skills, his commonsense approach to decision making and his unique ability to simplify designs which have led to many great products!"

—*Randy Watermiller, Director of Product Development*

Swing High Universally Accessible Playground,
Memorial Park, Colorado Springs, Colorado

Shane's
Inspiration
Building Common Ground®

"My dad was a bit of a 'mad scientist' at home. I remember finding TuffTurf®, a surfacing material in the freezer one day, and in the oven the next." —*Erin King, Steve and Barb's daughter*

Because other playground manufacturers are always quick to duplicate the materials, creative concepts and products we bring to the industry, we continually introduce new ideas and materials into our line of products. We're always moving ahead, and the evolution of our products will never end. For instance, we sat down and set guidelines for a new design; no decks and no straight posts. That's when we introduced Evos®, a playsystem that doesn't have decks, obvious points of entry or even straight lines in their design. Children have to create their own play patterns. Evos structures are made of steel arches that support a variety of events for climbing, jumping, sliding, spinning, hanging and whatever else children's imaginations suggest. Dozens of kids can play on an Evos structure at one time, and the experience can be different each time.

It seems as though we've done much of the research and development for the industry, and we know our ideas have been and will be copied. We learned a long time ago that in order to keep ahead of our competitors we have to be better and faster at developing new products. Because many of our products are "low tech," patents often don't mean much in our industry.

Transforming the culture of innovation

During the mid-1990s, Landscape Structures was expanding like crazy, and Barb and I knew we couldn't sustain that growth in our existing facilities for long. We saw a threat ahead. The way we were going, we would have to build a new building every two years to keep up with our growth. Our need for space was growing by 25,000 square feet a year. At the time, we were already operating three shifts. Things were about to sprawl in a big way, and we weren't sure that was the best direction to go. At the same time, we saw that too many of our orders went out wrong, and it took us 38 days to fill them. In our distribution center, we spent a lot of time just handling inventoried parts. We thought, "Wait a minute, there's got to be a better way to operate our business." Looking hard at our manufacturing process, we searched for ways to bring more efficiency to our operations.

(Left) Crossroads Elementary,
St. Paul, Minnesota

In short, we were searching for a transformation of our culture. That transformation began when we looked into the International Organization for Standardization (ISO) process, an internationally recognized measure of quality in manufacturing and customer service, as a way to improve the quality of our manufacturing. In 1996, we became the first U.S. playground equipment manufacturer to become ISO 9001 certified, meeting an internationally recognized standard for high quality. Two years later we earned ISO 14001 certification, becoming North America's first playground manufacturer—and only the third company in Minnesota—to meet rigorous standards of implementing an Environmental Management System intended to improve environmental performance. Landscape Structures employees have deservedly taken a great deal of pride and a feeling of ownership from these accomplishments. We've continued to meet even higher ISO standards in the years since.

During the next phase of our transformation, we studied lean manufacturing techniques. What would happen, we wondered, if we started manufacturing to order and stopped picking our products from an enormous inventory of parts?

It took me some time to understand all the implications of that change. It was the Kaizen approach to manufacturing that allowed us to enter that uncharted territory and carried us from delivering goods to our customers in 38 days to getting it done in two days. Kaizen is a Japanese word meaning *"change for the better,"* and it describes a process in which you continually improve every aspect of your business. We read about Toyota's implementation of Kaizen and how it saved time, space and money. Barb and I realized that we were ready to dedicate ourselves to the long and ongoing process of making Kaizen a part of our culture. What could be more entrepreneurial? So in 1999, we started the process.

We taught ourselves to become lean manufacturers. We began by working with consultants and benchmarking projects that showed us what other companies, like the furniture manufacturers Herman Miller and Foldcraft, had accomplished. Getting outside our own industry was something very important to Barb, and she had a real knack for finding great ideas and breakthroughs in the processes of other firms that were not our competitors. She was the one who began calling this phase of our history our "COOL journey"—with COOL standing for "Creating and recognizing Opportunities to improve, Opportunities to grow, Learning as we go and loving what we do."

Permalene® panels made from recycled/reclaimed post-consumer materials

Roll-forming machine used for Evos® and Weevos®

Concrete   Fabrication   Paint

PVC

Rotomold

Shipping

It was a huge change for us to develop the ability to manufacture to an order, not to draw from inventory. We had all kinds of questions about whether we could accomplish this. How would we catch up with our backlog of orders? When we no longer had a backlog, could we keep up with demand? Could we retrain and reorganize ourselves to have everyone working on the same job at the same time? After much work and effort, we found answers and were on our way.

We worked on developing our "Kaizen eyes" and challenging everything, especially our own beliefs of what we could achieve. It was about working smarter, not harder. During week-long Kaizen events, cross-functional teams would come together to improve a specific area or process. Many employees took part in improving the layout of work areas, building fixtures, eliminating setup time, studying the ergonomics of our work, designing new tools and procedures, keeping track of what worked and what didn't, reducing waste—we did whatever the team thought would bring improvement. In particular, we monitored our progress in improving such things as the amount of waste scrap we generated (down in value from $350,000 to $80,000 during the past decade), the time it took to change colors in our paint booth (20 minutes down to 90 seconds), the percentage of orders we accurately fulfilled (up to 99.8 percent from 86 percent in 2000), the time it took for us to produce and deliver orders and the savings we realized in manufacturing square footage—we even measured the distance our manufacturing employees walked on the job per month (down from 3.4 miles to 1.2 miles). We dropped down to a single work shift, and we brought tasks in-house that we used to outsource. As we've made all these gains, we managed to add product lines and equipment without erecting more buildings.

Through departmental meetings and interdepartmental brainstorming, we empowered employees to bring their ideas into the light. We totally upended our culture for the better. I don't think other playground equipment manufacturers have the culture to effectively imitate the gains Kaizen has brought us. You've got to have complete commitment to the process. Sometimes you've got to take people out of production for a week to solve a problem. Now the Kaizen approach is so inbred in our company that you couldn't pull it out no matter how hard you tried. We graduated from using lean manufacturing to having a lean enterprise.

(Left) Draw-forming machine creates various climbers

A big part of the process is moving decision-making out of the office and into the plant. The people who do the job will find better ways to do it. Low-hanging improvements came first, followed by more challenging changes. It took 18 months for us to make a pass through our plant from the front end of our manufacturing process through shipping. The Kaizen way of thinking assures you that you can change the process—and we evolved from batch manufacturing to making one playground at a time. It's a process that makes me feel as entrepreneurial as I did when we were first starting Landscape Structures.

We've since carried our lean thinking into our office and administrative areas: we practice lean accounting, which lets us focus on our activities that generate income rather than the dollars themselves, and we've learned how to do everything from ordering materials to producing product catalogs with greater efficiency and less expense. Everyone in the company took part in the effort to achieve change for the better, and they saw that we needed everybody's contributions—every employee could play a role in transforming Landscape Structures. It took us 10 years to make major changes.

When we won the Manufacturer of the Year Award from the Manufacturing Alliance in 2004, people really wanted to know how we had accomplished our transformation. The secret is in the commitment. Barb and I promised there would be no layoffs at Landscape Structures because of Kaizen. Our employees trusted that everyone would benefit from these changes. Now it's part of our culture, and the notion of change for the better circulates everywhere through our workplace. Everyone who tours our factory senses the immense pride that employees take in the process and in their work.

The biggest improvement we saw through Kaizen was in our culture. Some employees couldn't change, and they left by their own choice. We now have a team that's committed to making Landscape Structures as good as it can be, and people who want to contribute their full share. We worked together for a common cause. Numbers are easy to measure and improve, but the soft part of a business, the culture, is harder to strengthen. We survived hard recession years because of that culture.

PlayBooster® Vibe™,
Delano, Minnesota

We made important changes to our design and engineering process, as well. At the time, I was working with a lot of engineers. Engineers tend to be practical and think in straight lines and precise angles. One day I was voicing my concern about the need to make our products more "flowy." They wanted to know what I meant by "flowy," so I came up with a definition. They got it, and to this day, flowy is the focus of our design process. We now have a room in our Product Development department that we call the Flowy Room. Its sketch boards, tables and cabinet doors all exemplify the meaning of flowy.

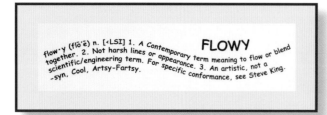

FLOWY

flow·y (flō'ē) n. [<LSI] 1. A Contemporary term meaning to flow or blend together. 2. Not harsh lines or appearance. 3. An artistic, not a scientific/engineering term. For specific conformance, see Steve King. -syn. Cool, Artsy-Fartsy.

Whether or not customers are aware of such improvements as flowy design, they have benefited from our many innovations in all facets of our business. The playstructures we produce are beautiful, safe, trend-setting and challenging. When customers ask to receive their order on a particular day, we are determined to make that happen, and the customer receives the order quickly, on time and accurately. Our vision of building one playground at a time has been achieved.

Life must be lived as play. — *Plato*

CHAPTER 3 Challenges and Opportunities

How Landscape Structures addresses and solves
challenges that kids (along with the rest of us) face today

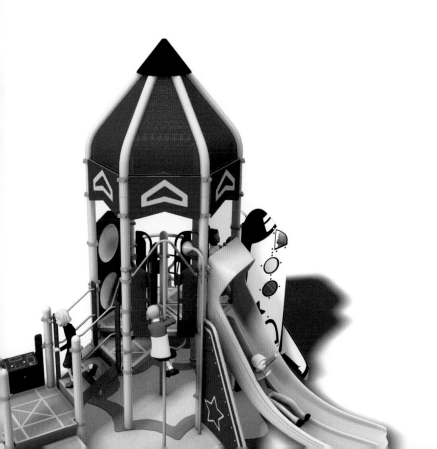

Inclusive play

CHALLENGE: How can we provide children of all abilities an opportunity to play together?

For decades, Landscape Structures has led the industry in the design of inclusive play environments. We create play environments in which all children and their families can play together, regardless of their abilities. We do this by providing an ever-expanding variety of play events that address accessibility, age and developmental appropriateness, and sensory-stimulating activity.

I've long been involved in advisory groups that have made accessibility recommendations for our industry and have set accessibility standards. I've seen us come a long way in providing access to playgrounds and to the play events on them. But experience tells me this isn't enough. Collectively, we need to look beyond ensuring access to ensuring inclusion. We need to continually ask ourselves, "Now that families are here, how can we increase their ability to enjoy and more fully take part in play activities?"

Recently, for example, we've been leading the way in designing play activities for those who have autism or those with Sensory Processing Disorder (SPD). (Read more details about SPD in Community Chapter 5). As recently as a dozen years ago, nobody knew much about the needs of children on the autism spectrum, and we now bring in specialists who can help find ways to deliver interesting activities to kids, enabling them to benefit from more intentional movement activities and sensory stimulation.

And we never forget the needs of parents and grandparents, because their presence is often critical to getting children outside in the first place, and helping them feel comfortable on the playground.

"Shane's Inspiration is forever grateful for the leadership of Steve and Barb King who inspired us to grow the dream of creating inclusive playgrounds for children of all abilities into a movement that is now reaching the far corners of the world. John Quincy Adams stated, 'If your actions inspire others to dream more, learn more, do more and become more, you are a leader.' Steve and Barb were living proof of this and their passion, commitment, integrity and joyful leadership have served as a beacon, guiding our journey since inception. Their legacy is extraordinary—both personally and professionally. We are blessed to have been sent the gift of such wise and generous souls."

—*Tiffany Harris, Co-Founder/CEO of Shane's Inspiration*

"Collectively, we need to look beyond ensuring access to ensuring inclusion. We need to continually ask ourselves, 'Now that families are here, how can we increase their ability to enjoy and more fully take part in play activities?'"—*Steve King*

The environment

CHALLENGE: For years, few playground equipment manufacturers emphasized recycled materials and the creative reuse of waste materials.

We have deep roots in environmental sustainability. It's part of who we are. Barb and I always lived with a focus on sustainability, and we brought that approach into the business.

We began focusing on environmental concerns in the early 1990s. One of our first efforts in using recycled materials was made from the conversion of plastic milk jugs into a textured "plastic lumber" that we used in our Alumacore® structures. As mentioned earlier, in 1998, we became the first commercial playground equipment manufacturer in North America to receive ISO 14001 certification for environmental leadership. The Kaizen process we adopted in the late 1990s (see Innovation Chapter 2) emphasizes efficiency and the reduction of waste. Recently, we took the lead in manufacturing environmentally sustainable playstructure components, such as panels from recycled materials.

La Mesa Park,
Santa Barbara, California

4th Avenue Park,
Avocado Heights, California

We also recycle all of the packaging materials we produce, but recycling is just the final option we consider in reducing our waste. With a true environmental focus, waste reduction starts upstream by reducing consumption and encouraging re-use. As a result, there is less material to recycle. Our concrete operations, for example, use filters to remove cement particles from the water we reuse. In the past, we disposed of those solids in a landfill. We now have found a way to actually repurpose those solids in our manufacturing, and we've reduced our consumption of filters and our disposal of landfill waste by 14,000 pounds a year. Using a similar approach, the welders in our machine shop replaced the grinding discs they long used to grind welds with higher performing discs that last longer, save time, save money and generate less solid waste. These benefits more than offset the slightly higher costs of the new discs.

So when the recent emphasis on "being green" happened, we didn't need to jump on the bandwagon. We were already on it, doing what we have done from the start. We love talking about the examples of sustainability you'll find at Landscape Structures. The best way we've found to communicate our daily focus on sustainability are the "Green Boards" in all of our manufacturing facilities. On these boards, employees can post updates on environmental challenges and share our progress in meeting environmental goals. We also publicly report our greenhouse gas emissions to the Climate Registry, and we partner with Global ReLeaf® to plant trees to offset our carbon emissions. As a result, we've received a great deal of recognition for our efforts to cut back on waste, including the Minnesota Waste Wise Leader Award.

Healthy kids

CHALLENGE: More than one-third of children and adolescents in America are obese. Childhood obesity has more than tripled during the past 30 years. Obesity leads to diabetes, heart disease, sleep apnea, bone disease and premature aging.

Landscape Structures' entire business focuses on making outdoor play challenging, fun and attractive to as many people as possible. Outdoor play must be more fun and attractive than video games.

Barb was so concerned about the rapid growth of childhood obesity that she founded the Säjai® Foundation, which fights the problem through a combination of educational programs for families, outreach to kids and community support. The Foundation reaches kids in after-school and summer programs to deliver the message that diet, active play, involvement with nature and the development of lifelong healthy habits can all contribute to overcoming obesity. The Foundation's staff and volunteers raise public awareness of the importance of a healthy lifestyle for children by organizing walks and other events, as well as by creating Wise Kids® program packs that make physical activity and play in nature fun for kids.

In addition, Landscape Structures is a longtime partner of Project Fit America, a nonprofit organization, that develops and donates fitness and physical education programs to schools. For decades, the company has designed and built fitness equipment for Project Fit America's programs, which in tandem with the organization's curriculum and on-site training at each school, are building an army of fit kids one school at a time.

Nature deficit

CHALLENGE: In decades past, the entire outdoor world was a child's playground. Kids hiked, explored, climbed trees, went fishing and swung on swings tied to branches. Now, due to urbanization, the concerns of parents, our car culture and other factors, fewer children have those opportunities for outdoor play. Some rarely venture far from home or school, and they suffer from "nature deficit"— a tragic unfamiliarity with the creative possibilities of playing outside.

Kids need nature. They need to spend time in natural places where they can get their hands into dirt, rocks, water and plants. Our intelligence is tied to what we learn as children, and playing in nature is a great learning experience.

In the equipment business, we cannot duplicate Mother Nature. But we can add water, sand and other natural elements. We can make equipment that is inspired by nature. We sculpt trees, mushrooms, logs and animals from concrete to look strikingly real. They blend well with the environment.

Some people might find it ironic that concrete is our medium for duplicating what's in nature. But this man-made material opens many creative possibilities that allow us to build replicas of the natural environment, including tree trunks, caves and boulders that meet safety regulations while giving kids the opportunity to climb, crawl and balance. Our logs, turtles and horses—we can create anything in our concrete plant—give kids a connection to these natural elements and some of the sensory stimulation that goes with it. Maybe we can't supply the bugs, grass or water that kids would find in nature, but almost every playground site can and should incorporate some of these natural features.

Lake Rebecca Park Reserve,
Rockford, Minnesota

Sunset Regional Park,
Clark County, Nevada

Safety

CHALLENGE : Current playground safety regulations discourage manufacturers like Landscape Structures from designing equipment that challenges kids to the fullest.

Playground safety has concerned me for a long time. In some ways, it's the most difficult part of our business. Highly skilled at designing safe playstructures, we manufacture equipment that has always complied with safety standards. But today's safety standards do not work well to safeguard children. As I mentioned in Chapter 1, I have spent more than 20 years on the ASTM committee that has the responsibility to set safety standards for public playgrounds.

The current state of regulation, litigation and over-protective safety standards means that we haven't been able to develop fun, yet challenging playground equipment for older kids, those 10 years old and older. We have dumbed down and sanitized our public playgrounds to the detriment of children.

The worst part of our business is the cost and time we spend on litigation. We receive several lawsuits every year, many of which are frivolous, from my perspective. I remember a lawsuit where a child was running toward the playground, and tripped on a tree root before he got there. The attorney accused us of providing an attractive nuisance. It cost us more than $50,000 to get out of that case. Legal defense, insurance and standards certification are now major expenses in our industry.

What can we change to make outdoor play more appealing to kids? Caregivers can take more responsibility. Safety standards can do more to take into account child development needs. The idea is to make playgrounds more attractive and challenging so kids play more often and stay longer.

Aeronet™ Climber

I'm concerned that we have driven kids indoors to play their video games or watch television. New playgrounds don't always have the value or challenge to keep them coming back. Meeting challenges and judging risks are important parts of growing up. Learning how to play, work together and resolve conflicts are an essential part of life. What better place to learn than on the playground?

The fact that children are injured using play equipment does not necessarily make the equipment dangerous or defective. Sometimes parents put kids on equipment not appropriate for their age. Kids run up slides. Kids jump off barriers. They climb to the highest part of a playstructure even if they're not supposed to. They push and shove. If the playstructure doesn't offer challenge, then kids will create their own. In other words, kids are being kids. Of all the accidents reported to us, none of them have involved play components that did not meet safety standards. Poor maintenance and lack of supervision account for most incidents.

We are never more fully alive, more completely

ourselves, or more deeply engrossed in anything,

than when we are at play. — *Charles Schaefer*

CHAPTER 4 Voices

In conversation about Landscape Structures

Company culture

"Once I gained experience in the working world, I realized how cool the environment at Landscape Structures was compared with most businesses. People have a good time and like their jobs. Now that I manage a business, I know how important and unusual that is."—*Adam King, Steve and Barb's son*

"We have always had an informal approach to management. We give people the responsibility with the authority to act. That's the hallmark of our company culture."—*Steve King*

"We don't make mistakes—we create opportunities. So you pick yourself up, you learn from it and go on, and you don't get bent out of shape."—*Barb King*

"One moment stays in my mind as an 'eye opening' experience that shows just who you are working for, and the normal kind of man Steve King is, and why this is such a great company. As a lead sprayer, I spent my days spraying panels that make up all of our Glass Fiber Reinforced Concrete (GFRC) rocks. A Kaizen was put together and Steve was among the group that would help lean out the current GFRC process and also determine pain points to avoid in the new concrete operations building. When it was time to learn the spray process, Steve jumped right in. He observed for just a moment and then insisted on trying out the spray gun. I'll always remember this because it showed Steve's dedication to know a process and understand everything down to the human component."
—*Cole Dehn, 3D Designer*

"We live the quest to improve every day. It's not just something management tells us. Coming up with ways to produce our products better, more environmentally friendly, quicker and less expensively has become part of our culture."—*Kristi Carlson, Director of Manufacturing*

"Working with Landscape Structures has been a wonderful marriage, and what we have *is* a marriage."
—*Eric O'Brien, Principal, M.E. O'Brien & Sons, Inc.*

"I still remember the first time I met Steve. It was my initial job interview. We had been talking for a while and I commented that it must be truly rewarding to build Landscape Structures from nothing to almost $50 million in sales and 180 employees. (I was trying to impress him by showing him I had done some research by reading an article in *Twin Cities Business Monthly* about Landscape Structures.) I asked how it felt to be so successful. He gave me that look that we have all seen at one time or another, and you can almost see his brain processing. And then you get hit with a question that stops you dead in your tracks and makes you have to think. He asked, 'Do these numbers really mean success?' With that question, I immediately realized I was sitting across from a true entrepreneur. His ideas had no limits, no preconceived definitions, no boundaries. And I knew I wanted to be a part of this culture."— *Bryan Sykora, Regional Sales Manager*

"I figured it out when I was a kid, growing up with Barb and Steve as parents. Even when Landscape Structures was a small company, they fostered the culture of an extended family. People are happy to work there and feel dedicated to seeing the company thrive. My mom always said that happy employees make better workers."—*Erin King, Steve and Barb's daughter*

"Landscape Structures has changed my life in so many different ways, but the biggest change was the night I asked my wife (16 years and still going) on a date while we were on first break, second shift, warehouse lunchroom, July 2, 1993. We now have two wonderful children and really have Steve and Barb to thank." —*Dave Johnson, Custom Products Engineer*

"Barb and Steve's announcement of an employee stock ownership plan emphasized that we have the talent and abilities in our employees to lead the industry. There's an amazing level of pride in our company, and everyone who tours our plant notices that. Employee ownership creates incredible unity and teamwork, and the enthusiasm you see on our shop floor is real, not fake. It was so reassuring to know that sharing the company with employees was the Kings' intention, rather than selling the company to someone else and just moving on." —*Pat Faust, President*

Quality and manufacturing

"The quality of Landscape Structures' products is very high. And the company is willing to adapt its designs in new ways so you don't just see the same old thing in play areas."—*Susan Goltsman, FASLA, Children's Environmental Designer, Principal, MIG, Inc.*

"We once had another playground equipment maker vying for our business. They made products that looked similar to Landscape Structures, and they donated some to a school that was in our program. The stuff rotted, rusted and had to be pulled out of the ground three years later. It can be more expensive to buy high-quality playground equipment, but it's a good investment for 20 or more years. Inferior equipment doesn't pass the test of time."—*Stacy Cook, Executive Director of Project Fit America*

"The quality of our products defines Landscape Structures. When I'm out driving, I often stop and look at playground equipment. I can tell from the road—our products look stronger and healthier. The pride we put in just jumps out."—*Ed Schaust, Production Activity Supervisor*

One of the many tools we have designed and built to give our products a consistent and high-quality appearance and also keep our employees safe.

"Improvement at Landscape Structures is not driven from the top down. We involve employees and let them make a difference." —*Michelle Krenik, ISO Safety Program Manager*

Paintline

Concrete paint finishing.

"One of the greatest things for me about working at Landscape Structures is the wide variety of roles available to me over my past 32 years here. One of the most gratifying and most challenging roles for me has been in supervising community playground builds. When supervising community builds, I get the pleasure of working with large groups of volunteers who have never built a playground before. Everyone involved gets a real sense of how a community effort can deliver an unexplainable sense of ownership and accomplishment. I believe the quality of our products and easy to read installation instructions make Landscape Structures the perfect fit for inexperienced volunteers who want to get involved making playground dreams come true for themselves and all of the children in their community."—*Randy Hartneck, PebbleFlex and Installation Services Manager*

"I think one of the greatest testaments to the Landscape Structures product is the fact that the St. Peter's School playground (in Delano, Minnesota) was there for more than 20 years, and was used by not only me as a child, but also my son. Considering that we both were able to enjoy playing on the playground is a true testament to the quality of our products."—*Nick Metz, Custom Products Presale Designer*

Play is our life

"I was a total playground snob as a kid. If the equipment didn't say Landscape Structures on it, I'd move on to the next park. I still do that to this day." —*Erin King, Steve and Barb's daughter*

"Here's the essence of play: get together, make up your own game, connect things, find your own challenge." —*Steve King*

"Barb loved to dance. I remember a trade show years ago when several of us went out to dance. All of a sudden, Barb got on my back, some other people jumped on other backs, and we were on the dance floor. The playful side of her was wonderful. You can imagine that this incident stretched my comfort zone."—*Fred Caslavka, Chief Financial Officer*

"I have worked at Landscape Structures for 15 years. When I started in 1997, we had three shifts. I have worked all of them, and loved every minute of it. When people ask me what I do for a job, I tell them I make playgrounds, and then ask the person if they make fun. When I go to work, I can say I make fun for kids." —*Ricky Plamann, Paintline Loader*

South Bowie Community Center,
Bowie, Maryland

Innovation

"When I first met Steve King, one of the things that most impressed me was his description of the 'Flowy Room' at Landscape Structures. This is the place in the company headquarters where people bounce ideas around, collaboration begins and creativity happens. It's so important for a company to give proper respect to the power of imagination."—*Dr. Gregory Geoffroy, President Emeritus of Iowa State University*

"Working in Product Development you better understand Steve's definition of the word 'Flowy.'"—*Steve Schaust, Product Development Project Manager*

"During a planning session we were trying to figure out what Landscape Structures' targeted lead time should be. Barb suddenly said, 'Two days!' Her words rang out and seemed to resonate through the whole business. Those words stuck. We all knew it was almost insane, but because of the success of previous Kaizen events we knew it was possible to get there." —*Tim Olson, Manufacturing Engineering Manager*

(Right) Mobius® Climber

Penny Park, Silver City, New Mexico

"In 2005, Steve spoke at the International meeting about a PlayBooster® post for an hour. It was so interesting. Any time Steve talks about the Landscape Structures history or our products, he holds your attention."—*Pat Tacheny, Playground Designer*

"Our vision is to be innovation leaders in our industry. Innovation has been in us since Steve and Barb started. To me it's obvious that's what we have always been about."—*Pat Faust, President*

"I will always be amazed by how accurate Steve's 'gut feel' reactions have been over the years, and his constant reminders to all of the engineers the importance of 'flowy' design."—*Randy Watermiller, Director of Product Development*

(Left) Penny Park, Silver City, New Mexico

You can discover more about a person in an

hour of play than in a year of conversation. — *Plato*

CHAPTER 5 Community

"It's important in any community to create a place where everyone can meet and mix, and I look at those projects as some of our best." —*Steve King*

It's magical

when a playground sits at the heart of a community, serving as a place where neighbors, friends and strangers of all ages spend time together. At times, the playground can serve as a meeting place, especially for young families.

How often has one mother told another, "Let's get together at the park with the kids at 2:00?" Teens hang out at playgrounds long after they've outgrown the equipment, because of the good memories they have.

Playgrounds draw not only children and families, but also dog walkers, runners and bikers who need a rest, groups that want to meet outdoors to discuss issues of the day and folks who just want a spot to read and daydream.

Carnfunnock Country Park,
Larne, Northern Ireland

Every playground should serve its community. Not every one of our playstructures can claim such a prized status in its neighborhood, but we love the ones that do. That's why I often tell myself that playgrounds are great for the whole community, not just for children. Everyone at Landscape Structures understands this. Our multi-generational approach springs naturally from our continuous play concept—using our original philosophy to solve the challenges of designing great spaces for the entire community.

Communities of many generations

In recent years, we have purposefully designed play environments that appeal to many generations of people, from infants to senior citizens. It's important in any community to create a place where everyone can meet and mix, and I look at those projects as some of our best. We're seeing increasing numbers of playgrounds built at senior housing complexes because senior citizens enjoy watching children play. We also are seeing an increase in our HealthBeat® outdoor fitness system in these environments.

Community Build at Big Rock Park,
Delano, Minnesota

Building together

Communities take extra pride and ownership in their playgrounds when neighbors help construct and maintain them. Landscape Structures has supported community builds—events in which people join together to unpack and assemble playstructures, sometimes completing the task in a single day—for decades. These events started a revolution in strengthening communities, and they've been especially popular since the 1990s. We now provide detailed plans for community builds. We've seen neighborhoods change as a result of the process. When you join all of your neighbors to build a playground, you establish lifelong relationships. You get to know people from blocks around and share pride in the terrific playground you've all built.

Partners in the community

Beyond the playground, Landscape Structures plays another important role in building communities. We've formed partnerships with many health, fitness and play-focused organizations in the past, and we've learned a great deal from those collaborations. We're happy to have an incredible partnership with Shane's Inspiration®, a nonprofit international organization dedicated to designing inclusive playgrounds and programs that eliminate bias against children with disabilities, diminishing the bullying and exclusion that these children often face. We are proud to be working with Shane's Inspiration to expand its programming across North America through the distribution of the Inclusion Lunchbox® education program. The Together, We Are Able® education program, launched in 2004, reduces the social isolation of children with disabilities by educating their peers in classroom workshops and by connecting children with different abilities on the playground.

Most recently we have supported the Sensory Processing Disorder (SPD) Foundation and its Sensory Therapies and Research (STAR) Center in Greenwood Village, Colorado, which advocates and conducts research for children with SPD, a neurological condition in which sensory messages are misinterpreted by the brain. Children with SPD need help in building their social skills, self-regulation and self-esteem, and the STAR Center, with the support of Landscape Structures, is launching an initiative to provide that assistance using the playground as a natural setting in which to accomplish therapeutic goals. We have designed for them a collection of innovative outdoor playstructures that offer many different kinds of sensory-based and socializing-play experiences. These are similar to sensory-based playstructures that we offer to schools, childcare centers and city parks.

Partnerships like these bring us recognition from the communities we serve. In our home of Wright County, Minnesota, the region's Economic Development Partnership gave us its Outstanding High-Economic Vitality Business of the Year award in 2009, partly in recognition of our dedication to community involvement. But all across the world, our playstructures contribute to the dynamism of their communities. You can detect it in the sounds, bonds, experiences and memories they create.

(Top) STAR Center,
Greenwood Village, Colorado

(Bottom)
Shane's Inspiration
Fairmount Carousel Playground,
Riverside, California

Shane's
Inspiration
Building Common Ground®

Renee's Place
Pan Pacific Park,
Los Angeles, California

Every Child Deserves a Chance to Play Baseball

"Upon meeting Barb and Steve King for the first time in 2007, I knew that their passion to bring play to all children was something The Miracle League wanted to be a part of. Since the first installation of our first Miracle League Playground in 2007, I recognized that a Miracle League Complex couldn't be complete without a Landscape Structures playground. But then I was reminded when I received a phone call from a gentleman with deep emotions, explaining to me his appreciation to The Miracle League and Landscape Structures for developing a playground so ALL could play. He began to tell me his story of how he was wounded in Iraq and left with no legs. He stated that it was very difficult for him to be able to play with his small children. But this team made up of Landscape Structures and The Miracle League had made it happen! He was now able to roll into the playground and play with his children. 'This was priceless,' he stated. So many times when you do things for all the right reasons you touch people without recognizing the difference you truly make—that's who Barb and Steve King are.

There are experiences that change the way we look at life, the way we pursue our dreams and the way we live our lives. The Miracle League and Landscape Structures' playgrounds are one of these experiences." —*Diane Alford, International Executive Director, The Miracle League*

(Left) Homer, the official mascot of The Miracle League

One community in Zambia

Community builds are part of our blood. In 2012, I took a trip to the village of Chiawa in Zambia, in the southern third of Africa. While there, I helped plan their first-ever playground for their school and community. They desperately need an outdoor learning environment for their children—a place where kids can stay active and find a purpose. This playground will improve children's health and teach them how to work, plan, play and resolve conflicts together. People in the community will build and maintain the structure.

"I realized that this is what I was doing back in 1970 with pencils, paper, wood and an opportunity."—*Steve King*

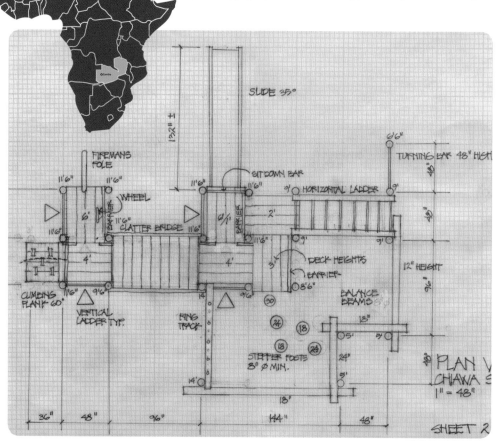

Without technology or any fancy devices, I began designing playstructures for the people in Chiawa built from native wood, the most plentiful building material available there. As I worked, I realized that this is what I was doing back in 1970 with pencils, paper, wood and an opportunity. Using those ingredients, I made solutions that helped kids, families, schools, parks and communities. And here I was doing it again—the old way. For me, the challenges and satisfactions of my life's work have never changed.

Play has been man's most useful preoccupation. —*Frank Caplan*

EPILOGUE

Letter written and read by employee Tom Zanoth, PVC Material Handler, for the 2005 Landscape Structures Sales Meeting

ESOP, as many of you know, stands for Employee Stock Ownership Plan. And to each and every individual here, it means something different.

But, I'm here today to tell you what it means to me. We are all very special people. Beginning with Steve and Barb, to all of the executive officers, and all the different departments that help support Landscape Structures, to our supervisors, park rangers and team leads, right down to us employees. We are all special and each play an important role in our company. And that's why we love working here; we're just one big happy family.

Now I wish to tell you a story. One that had such an impact on my life, I will never forget. About five years ago, in September, I was hired as a temp as a material handler here at Landscape Structures and I was so excited to work here. All I knew was that they made playground equipment. On my very first day, everyone made me feel welcome, that it made me happy, and I can think of a lot of friends that just did that. I could feel the excitement in me every day that I got up, because I take pride in what I do and still continue to do. I loved going to work and supplying the paintline with parts to build playground equipment.

Soon it was December, my first company Christmas party, where all of the sales reps would be there, from all over. I was really excited. We walked all around yelling, screaming and cheering at the reps, to welcome them to our party.

I can also remember when one of you reps came up to me and asked, "What do you do?" I told him I was a material handler for the paintline and had to go outside to get different lengths of pipe, for the many types of playstructures. I even had to go out in the cold, in a snowstorm when it was 20 below. And I tell you what he said to me. "Do it for the kids, our kids, who play on all the different kinds of playground equipment." And from that day on I enjoyed working at Landscape Structures even more. So knowing we have a responsibility to those kids and being part-owner, makes me and I'm sure, all of you here at Landscape Structures, very happy. Happy that we're doing it for all the children, all over the world, who play on Landscape Structures' playground equipment. Because it's all about you, the reps, each and every one of you for selling our Landscape Structures equipment. And I know you knew all of this time that we are doing this for our children who are and will continue to play on Landscape Structures' equipment.

And besides, I'm proud to wear a cap that says: Landscape Structures, an employee-owned company.

Thank you.

"We have Barb and Steve to thank for enriching the lives of each employee who works here. There are many examples of their generosity over the years, but I would have to say that each of us felt a great sense of pride in this company the day that Barb and Steve decided to make Landscape Structures ours through an ESOP!" —*Sheryl Theisen, Master Planner*

Landscape Structures Employees (as of 12/2012)

A

Abfalter, Ann
6/27/2011

Anderson, Cory
3/3/2008

Anderson, Dawn
8/2/2000

Anderson, Doug
6/24/2002

Anderson, Jared
5/21/2008

Anderson, Jeff
12/18/2006

Anderson, Sam
1/31/2011

Andrada, Megan
7/25/2005

Andrews, Lisa
8/26/1996

B

Balboa, Ruben
8/23/1999

Bardahl, Craig
5/26/2008

Barfnecht, Michelle
11/25/2002

Barrera-Quintana, Bonifacio
11/14/2000

Barrett, Tim
12/1/2003

Bartels, Lynn
2/1/1996

Baumann, Tim
3/3/1986

Becker, Rick
7/2/2007

Beckrich, Andrew
5/10/2010

Beise, Justin
4/2/2007

Benzing, Jason
8/25/2008

Berge, Tina
12/9/2002

Bergeron, Tony
9/29/2008

Bernardi, Giovanni
9/19/2011

Bigalke, Mike
8/31/1981

Bistodeau, Tracy
9/24/2010

Borden, Sarah
8/31/2012

Borg, Carol
1/30/1995

Borgia, Julian
10/1/2012

Borne, Kristin
6/20/2005

Brey, Christine
6/4/2001

Brey, Lucas
5/22/2006

Burns, David
1/22/2007

C

Carlson, Kristi
7/12/2000

Caslavka, Fred
7/1/1991

Chavez-Segobiano, Rigoberta
11/15/2000

Christensen, Nick
3/10/1997

Clark, Kris
3/31/2008

Cole, Michael
4/23/2012

Connelly, John
9/10/2001

Cotten, Gabriel
6/23/2008

Cruz, Nicolas
5/29/2003

D

Dahlin, Bruce
1/10/2000

Dahlstrom, Jim
2/6/2006

Dawson, Bruce
9/23/1991

Dawson, Mary
7/31/2002

Decker, Carolyn
4/24/1989

Dehn, Cole
10/29/2007

Demars, Ryan
5/28/1999

Dolezal, Dan
8/14/1999

Dressel, Steve
10/5/1997

Duffy, Al
4/9/1990

Duffy, Shelley
12/17/1991

Duske, Ben
11/8/1999

Dye, Mike
11/17/2008

Dye, Tim
12/20/1999

E

Elfmann, Jessica
9/28/2009

Emerson, Karlye
11/19/2001

Erickson, James
4/30/2012

F

Fadden, Robin
7/10/2000

Faulkner, Dorothy
6/15/2009

Faust, Pat
10/3/1994

Fawley, Matt
8/24/1999

Fetzer, Lindsay
5/28/2012

Fiereck, Mike
6/4/2003

Fingeroth, Mike
3/12/2012

Fitzpatrick, Tom
2/4/2002

Fuller, Bill
9/20/2011

G

Galvin, Sara
8/25/2008

Gartner, Stefanie
5/21/2012

Gassman, Troy
4/23/2001

Glaeser, Jason
8/26/2002

Gosswiller, Tim
4/10/1995

Gouge, Jeremie
4/30/2012

Grahn, Ron
10/15/1990

Gray, Jenny
3/10/2003

Gray, Lorie
6/4/2001

Gray, Mike
11/1/2012

Green, Ryan
6/11/2007

Gregory, Ken
10/22/2012

Grengs, Terry
5/8/1990

Grenzer, Ben
5/29/2007

Griffin, Tristen
10/19/2009

Griggs, Kim
1/15/1992

Grimm, Michael
6/28/2004

Grittman, Ryan
5/3/2010

Grochow, Dave
5/7/1990

Grossman, Mary Ellen
4/30/2004

Gruette, Gerald
7/26/1989

Gunderson, Gus
12/14/1987

Gunnarson, Peter "Gunnar"
11/14/2008

Gunnerson, Tyler
7/2/2012

Gunter, Rock
12/19/2005

Gutierrez-Lopez, Nieves
4/12/1999

H

Hackenmueller, Tonya
8/1/2008

Haeg, Christa
6/29/2012

Hagberg, Dan
6/23/2010

Haire, Jesse
8/1/2008

Haley, Wendy
7/15/1985

Hall, Nikki
11/20/2006

Hare, Steve
10/1/2007

Harkness, Elaine
3/26/1997

Harris, Harold
3/3/2008

Hartneck, Randy
9/30/1980

Hayes, Jean
7/15/1985

Henrichs, Alex
1/31/2011

Heuer, Tom
5/11/1997

Hickle, Tyler
8/31/2012

Hicks, Perry
3/12/1990

Hiller, Dan
2/8/1982

Hoffman, Wes
6/4/2001

Holland, Travis
12/1/2009

Holte, Wayne
10/4/1993

Huehn, Jonathan
2/1/2010

Hurley, Tom
3/31/2000

I

Isaacs, Dan
5/12/2008

J

Jackson, Dan
12/14/1987

Jackson, Matt
5/30/2001

Jacobson, Rich
11/18/1997

Jenewein, Jane
3/3/2003

Johnson, Dave
6/1/1990

Johnson, Jeff
2/21/2005

Jolicoeur, Lisa
3/1/2010

Jordan, Karen
11/10/2008

K

Kaiser, Jeff
4/14/1980

Kaiser, Lowell
5/24/2004

Kane, Steve
11/24/2008

Kangas, Kevin
12/12/2011

Kangas, Mark
9/26/2001

Karhatsu, Peter
3/3/2008

Kava, Katie
1/16/2006

Keck, Gene
5/14/1979

Keller, Tom
1/12/2004

Kelly, Tim
6/9/2011

Kieffer, Earl
9/24/2001

King, Steve
4/1/1971

Kirshbaum, Steve
12/30/2004

Kolkman, Noah
12/1/2009

Kotilinek, Dan
3/1/2010

Kowalski, Marie
2/21/1978

Kraml, Greg
1/11/2010

Krause, Robert
3/18/1997

Kreitz, Danah
11/1/2012

Krenik, Michelle
6/15/1987

Kronback, Mike
5/12/2003

Kruchowski, Nick
12/22/2011

Kuhnau, Don
9/12/1994

Kwilinski, Tjaart
11/22/2004

L

Lambert, Chad
10/29/2007

Leffew, Connie
2/5/2007

Liljenberg, Sue
8/16/1999

Luebke, Mark
2/1/2010

M

Macht, Nicole
8/8/2011

Madson, Amy Jo
12/17/1999

Magnuson, Pat
6/20/1994

Majerus, Larry
3/25/2002

Maki, Erik
10/12/1998

Marketon, Erica
10/23/2000

Martens, Steve
3/29/1999

Martinez, Jose
2/9/2009

Matter, Lori
2/17/1987

Mattis, Al
10/11/2004

Matuseski, Mark
5/27/2008

McClure, Chad
3/30/2009

McConkey, John
10/15/2002

McDill, Sue
4/23/2012

McLain Miller, Karen
11/1/2000

Meester, Lee
6/3/1998

Meffert, John
8/28/1989

Mellgren, Brian
12/15/1997

Mellgren, Nick
5/23/2011

Menk, Jody
8/20/1990

Menth, Miranda
5/16/2007

Metz, Nick
6/21/1999

Metz, Robert
12/19/2011

Meyer, Greg
3/15/2004

Miller, David
8/31/2012

Mochinski, Joanie
12/19/2005

Mochinski, Ryan
10/25/2010

Moonen, Paul
5/8/1989

Moore, Jared
11/1/2012

Mulhollam, Matt
6/13/2011

Myers, Chris
9/29/2008

Myrmel, Kyle
10/16/2006

N

Norlin, Zach
2/21/2011

Nowacki VanDenheuvel, Jessica
8/13/2007

Nowak, Steve
6/15/1998

Nyquist, Aaron
3/19/2007

O

O'Brien, Tracy
2/21/2011

Obrecht, Mark
7/16/2007

Olson, Bob
5/31/1998

Olson, Ken
3/26/2001

Olson, Tim
7/18/1999

Osberg, Derek
9/29/2008

P

Palaia, Matt
3/9/2009

Paulson, Ben
9/29/2008

Pawelk, Jesse
10/29/2007

Pedersen, Sheri
7/14/2008

Peppin, Paul
2/8/1982

Picton, Steve
8/31/2012

Pinoniemi, Lynn
1/11/2002

Plager, Steven
11/30/2009

Plamann, Ricky
6/28/1998

Pohl, Dan
3/17/2008

Price, Luke
10/1/2010

Prinsen, Sally
9/18/2006

Provo, Nick
5/3/2010

Puente, Jorge
3/29/1999

Puma, Marcello
3/8/2004

R

Rasset, Corey
5/31/2007

Reich, Stacey
12/12/2008

Reider, Jon
12/18/2008

Robins, Marty
1/16/2012

Roepke, Scott
7/2/2007

Roff, Tory
9/15/2008

Rogalski, Dan
3/1/2010

Rome, Brian
2/21/2011

Roschi, Scott
6/20/2011

Rose, Bill
3/1/2011

Ruacho, Jose
2/28/2000

Ruhland, Jay
12/23/2009

Ruiz, Diego
11/8/1999

Rumpza, Brian
6/6/1987

Ruthenberg, Susan
5/17/2004

Ryks, Trevor
2/8/2000

S

Saluti, Jerry
9/16/2011

Saluti, Rose
9/16/2011

Sanchez, Carlos
7/11/1999

Sawatzke, Jan
11/30/1998

Schaust, Brian
1/28/1985

Schaust, Ed
5/21/1979

Schaust, Steve
3/18/1980

Schemenauer, Eric
4/2/2007

Schmidt, Darci
8/25/1998

Schramel, Stacey
6/30/1997

Schrein, Allison
5/21/2012

Schwankl, Ed
10/23/1989

Seager, Jon
3/24/2003

Sinnamon, Howard
5/29/2001

Sipert, Herbert
4/1/2008

Smith, David
2/12/2010

Smith, Steve
11/26/2001

Smith, Tim
7/2/2012

Spooner, Roger
3/1/2001

Spurbeck, Jonathan
12/20/2001

Stahn, Dan
11/1/2007

Stein, Jack
9/1/2010

Stelton, Dave
9/14/1992

Stender, Nathan
4/30/2012

Stender, Tammy
6/29/1998

Stremick, Wayne
5/21/1998

Sundberg, Jory
10/26/2009

Suska, Brock
6/21/1999

Sykora, Bryan
6/5/1995

T

Tacheny, Pat
9/29/2000

Tessman, Lloyd
5/1/1993

Teubert, Chad
11/13/2000

Theisen, Lonnie
2/19/1986

Theisen, Sheryl
1/20/1997

Thorson, Ryan
4/28/2000

Topel, Fred
4/9/2001

Tormanen, Kathy
10/17/1994

Trainor, Bob
8/26/1997

Trittabaugh, Gregg
6/12/1995

U

Ungaro, Nick
4/15/2002

Usueta, Adelaido
11/16/1998

V

Van Erp, Jason
9/3/2007

Venstad, Wade
12/1/2009

Vermilya-Jacobson, Janith
1/22/2007

W

Walker, Kara
2/7/2000

Watermiller, Randy
6/19/1989

Wendorff, Jeanette
3/15/1991

West, Ryan
8/1/2002

Wetter, Tom
3/9/1992

Whited, Faye
11/1/2012

Wiegert, Cheryl
12/22/1997

Williams, Holly
4/29/2005

Wilson, Gary
1/3/2002

Wilson, Patrick
1/2/2007

Winterhalter, Erwin
3/2/1987

Winterhalter, Willie
9/25/1989

Witter, Mark
8/31/2012

Woitalla, Daniel
11/1/2012

Workman, Pam
9/29/1997

Wrolson, Darryl
11/22/2010

Wuollet, Tony
6/30/2008

Wysocki, Will
11/17/2008

Z

Zanoth, Steve
8/1/2008

Zanoth, Tom
4/8/2002

Zitzloff, Dawn
2/13/1991

Landscape Structures Sales Representatives

North America Sales Representatives and start dates

A.B.C. Recreation LTD.
2/1/1992

ACS Playground Adventures
8/29/2007

Architectural Design Specialties
3/1/2011

Arkoma Playgrounds & Supply, LLC
6/1/1996

ATHCO, L.L.C.
11/17/1975

Carolina Parks & Play, LLC
5/1/2010

Coast Recreation, Inc.
3/12/1993

Countryside Play Structures, LLC
12/5/2008

Creative Play
6/12/2007

Dakota Fence
7/28/1977

DYNA-PLAY, L.L.C.
8/1/2005

ExerPlay, Inc.
11/8/1990

Flagship Recreation
12/1/2009

General Recreation, Inc.
9/1/1984

Gerber Leisure Products, Inc.
10/20/1975

Habitat Systems Inc.
6/1/1996

Island Recreation
1/2/2003

Lone Star Recreation, Inc.
4/15/1995

NuToys Leisure Products, Inc.
1/16/1976

O'Brien & Sons, Inc.
6/1/1981

Outdoor Recreation Products
2/5/1982

Parkitects, Inc.
9/1/1996

PlayCreation, Inc.
9/30/2004

PLAYGROUNDS-R-US
1/20/1999

PLAYSCAPES
1/2/2009

Recreation Consultants of Texas
11/1/1999

RecWest Outdoor Products, Inc.
1/2/1993

Rep Services, Inc.
8/9/1990

Rocky Mountain Recreation Inc.
5/24/1994

Ross Recreation Equipment Company, Inc.
10/29/1974

Service Supply Ltd., Inc.
9/1/1984

Site Specialists Ltd.
2/27/2003

Sonntag Recreation, LLC
2/24/1981

Sparks@Play, LLC
12/1/2008

Superior Play, L.L.C.
4/3/2006

International Sales Representatives and start dates

Amaco United Group
3/15/1988

American Eastern Dubai LLC
11/8/1988

Crawford Group
11/3/2003

Giochisport
4/1/1992

GreenBuild Infra Pvt Ltd.
11/1/2011

JUMBO
7/2/2007

KOTOBUKI CORPORATION
3/23/1982

Microarquitectura
6/1/2007

Playscape Creations
1/2/2009

Retro-Max PTE LTD
9/24/1998

Samson Urban Elements B.V.
7/27/2012

Toptech Co. Limited
6/1/1981

"I met Steve 30 years ago in Delano, Minnesota, as part of a trip to meet with several playground equipment manufacturers in Europe and the U.S. Steve and Barbara were very young, and had just started making playground equipment using redwood a few years prior. Steve invited me to a small café for sandwiches and then to his home. I remember clearly that he showed me his 'wood station' on the way. His enthusiasm, innovative thinking and design compelled me to work with him rather than develop playground equipment myself in Japan. We became one of the first companies to import from Landscape Structures, and in some years we were also their largest importer. Our partnership helped us become the leading supplier of playground equipment in Japan.

I'm glad I decided to partner with Steve as it has contributed to our mutual success over the years. I was saddened by Barbara's passing a few years ago, but I believe she and Steve spent a very happy 40 years together building a home and company together. I am sure that Steve's entrepreneurial spirit, reliability and innovative thinking will serve as a good example for the next generation." —*Shigeyuki Fukasawa, Chairman, KOTOBUKI CORPORATION*

"In May of 1991, I was invited to Minneapolis for the first time, and I had no idea that would be the turning point in my life. Meeting Barb and Steve really left their mark on me. Starting from the very first day we spent together in Steve's boat on Lake Minnetonka, I realized we had more in common than simply two creative and innovative businessmen.

I remember that afternoon we went home to meet Barb and have a cup of tea; their dog stayed by me the whole time. Barb said, 'Our dog only looks for good people.' From that moment on we created a long-lasting relationship. When I think about Barb I feel an emptiness, but I am convinced, wherever she is now, she still is inspiring and directing part of the work.

The vision of Landscape Structures and innovative playgrounds have an explosive force that goes far beyond the parks they create: it's introduced a real cultural shift of play and its connection with children. All is new and forward at Landscape Structures: its park vision, the respect for the environment, the love for the planet, the sense of its creation, the concept of 'continuous play.' Giochisport has always loved this vision." —*Angelo Bongiorno, President, Giochisport*

The King Pavilion at
Iowa State University, Ames, Iowa

An addition to the College of Design
dedicated in August 2009

Steve King and family at the dedication of the King Pavilion
(left to right)
Evalyn, Adam, Tara, Charlotte, Steve, Isabelle, Erin and Mark